Nita Mehta's

Saatvik K

Delicious Food without Onion & Garlic

Nita Mehta

B.Sc. (Home Science), M.Sc. (Food and Nutrition), Gold Medalist

Co-Author
Sugandha Aggarwal

SNAB
Excellence in Books

Nita Mehta's

Saatvik Khaana
Delicious Food without Onion & Garlic

SNAB
Excellence in Books
Snab Publishers Pvt Ltd

Corporate Office
3A/3, Asaf Ali Road, New Delhi 110 002
Phone: +91 11 2325 2948, 2325 0091
Telefax: +91 11 2325 0091
E-mail: nitamehta@nitamehta.com
Website: www.nitamehta.com

© Copyright SNAB PUBLISHERS PVT LTD 2012
All rights reserved

ISBN 978-81-7869-354-5

First Print 2012

Printed in India at Infinity Advertising Services (P) Ltd, New Delhi

Contributing Writers:
Anurag Mehta
Tanya Mehta
Subhash Mehta

Editors :
Sangeeta
Sunita

Distributed by :
NITA MEHTA BOOKS
3A/3, Asaf Ali Road, New Delhi - 02

Distribution Centre :
D16/1, Okhla Industrial Area, Phase-I,
New Delhi - 110020
Tel.: 26813199, 26813200
E-mail: nitamehta.mehta@gmail.com

Editorial and Marketing office
E-159, Greater Kailash II, New Delhi 110 048

Food Styling and Photography by Snab
Typesetting by National Information Technology Academy
3A/3, Asaf Ali Road, New Delhi 110 002

Recipe Development & Testing:
Nita Mehta Foods - R & D Centre
3A/3, Asaf Ali Road, New Delhi - 110002

Price: Rs. 99/-

Introduction

In India there are certain days in a year when people do not eat onions and garlic. In some of the festivals also, people prepare food without onion and garlic. This book would be very helpful to those who follow religions like Jainism, Radhaswami and also people who are vegetarians and do not like to consume onion and garlic. All the recipes in this book were tried and tested by our kitchen team and we found that without onion and garlic also the food tastes really good. Drinks like cool flavor and khus punch also came out very well. Indian, Chinese and Continental snacks were also delicious. You will love cooking gravies, dry vegetables, paranthe, rice and preparing mouthwatering desserts in your kitchen for your family.

Nita Mehta

Contents

WHAT'S IN A CUP?
INDIAN CUP: 1 teacup = 200 ml liquid
AMERICAN CUP: 1 cup = 240 ml liquid (8 oz.)
The recipes in this book were tested with the Indian teacup which holds 200 ml liquid.

Drinks

Cool Flavor

Serves 2

2 cups cold milk
2 tbsp kesar-pista Ice cream
½ cup vanilla ice cream
4 tbsp badam bahar syrup or thandai syrup
1 tsp powdered sugar
some ice cubes
2 tbsp faluda

GARNISH
1 tbsp chopped almonds
1 tbsp chopped pistachios
1 tbsp chopped cashew nuts
1 tbsp fresh pomegranate kernels

1. Pour milk, kesar-pista ice cream, vanilla ice cream, badam bahar syrup, sugar and ice cubes in a mixer and blend 2-3 times.

2. Put falooda in a tall glass. Pour the blended milk.

3. Garnish with cashewnuts, pistachio, fresh pomegranate and serve.

Cold Coffee Special

Serves 2

100 gms vanilla ice cream
2 cups cold milk
4 tsp coffee powder
1 tbsp powdered sugar
some ice cubes

GARNISH

¼ tsp cocoa powder

1. Pour all the ingredients in a mixer and blend nicely.

2. Pour in a glass and sprinkle cocoa powder on top.

3. Your cold coffee is ready.

Rose Tall Drink

Serves 2

1 bottle (3 cups) 7 up/sprite (600 ml)
¼ cup rose syrup
1 tbsp lemon juice
1 cup vanilla ice cream
some ice cream

GARNISH
4-5 rose petals

1. Put all the ingredients in a mixer and blend nicely.

2. Pour in a tall glass, garnish with rose petals and serve.

Orange Delight

Serves 2

1½ cups Mirinda
1 tbsp rose syrup or rooh afza
1 tbsp lemon juice
2 pinches salt
½ tsp powdered sugar
½ cup vanilla ice cream
some ice cubes

1.   Blend all ingredients together in a mixer.
2.   Pour into glasses and serve.

Khus Punch

Serves 1

1 cup chilled water
juice of ½ lemon
2 pinches of black salt (*kala namak*)
3 tbsp powdered sugar
2 tsp khus syrup

GARNISH
2 tsp grated apple

1. Mix all the ingredients in a mixer and blend together.

2. Pour in a glasses and serve topped with grated apple.

Snacks

Stuffed Khandvi

Makes 9-10

½ cup gram flour (*besan*)
½ cup curd - mixed with 1 cup water to get
1½ cups butter milk)
¼ tsp turmeric (*haldi*) powder
½ tsp cumin (*jeera*) powder
½ tsp coriander (*dhaniya*) powder
a pinch of asafoetida (*hing*)
1 tsp salt

GINGER-GREEN CHILLY PASTE
2 green chillies and 1½ tsp chopped ginger -
grind in a mixer to a paste

FILLING
1 tbsp oil
1 tsp mustard seeds (*rai*)
1 tbsp chopped raisins (*kishmish*)
1 tbsp chopped fresh coriander
1 tbsp grated carrot
2 tbsp grated fresh coconut
¼ tsp salt

CHOWNK (TEMPERING)
1½ tbsp oil
1 tsp mustard seeds (*rai*)
1 green chilly - chopped finely

GARNISH
1 tbsp finely chopped fresh coriander
1 tbsp grated coconut

1. Mix gram flour with 1½ cups butter milk till smooth. Add turmeric, cumin powder, coriander powder, asafoetida, salt and ginger-green chili paste.

2. Spread a cling film (plastic sheet) on the backside of a big tray.

3. Keep the mixture on low heat in a non stick pan. Cook this mixture for about 10-12 minutes, stirring, till the mixture becomes very thick and translucent.

4. Drop 1 tsp of mixture on the tray and spread. Let it cool for a few seconds and check if it comes out easily. If it does, remove from fire, otherwise cook for another 5 minutes. Remove from fire.

5. While the mixture is still hot, quickly spread some of the mixture as thinly and evenly as possible on the cling film. Level it with a knife or the back of a steel *katori*.

6. For the filling, heat oil. Add mustard seeds. After it crackles, add coconut, carrot, raisins, and chopped coriander. Add salt. Mix. Remove from fire.

7. After the gram flour mixture cools, cut breadth wise into 2" wide strips. Put 1 tsp filling at one end of a strip. Roll strip, loosening with a knife initially, to get small cylinders. Repeat with all strips.

8. Prepare the tempering by heating oil in a small vessel. Add mustard seeds. When mustard splutters, add green chillies. Remove from fire and pour the oil on the khandvis arranged in the plate. Garnish with coconut and coriander.

Corn Cutlet

Makes 14-15

1 cup boiled or frozen corns
5 medium sized potatoes - boiled, peeled and mashed, ½ cup grated carrot
1 tsp butter, 1 tsp grated ginger
1½ salt, ¼ tsp (8-10) black pepper corns (*saboot kali mirch*), 1 tsp dry mango powder (*amchoor*)
½ tsp chaat masala
½ tsp curd, 2-3 tbsp cornflour
¾ cup dry bread crumbs
oil for frying

1. Grind half of the corns in a grinder and squeeze with both hands. Keep the whole corns aside.

2. In a pan heat butter. Add ginger and sauté. Add carrot, mashed potatoes, corns (ground and whole), salt, pepper corns, dry mango powder and chaat masala. Mix well. Saute for 4-5 minutes.

3. Remove from fire. Cool the mixture. Add curd and cornflour and mix well. Make small sized cutlets and roll in bread crumbs. Keep in refrigerator for ½ an hour.

4. Heat oil in a pan. Fry cutlets till golden brown. Serve hot with sauce or chutney.

Shehanshahi Dahi Bade

Makes 40

1½ cup plain flour (*maida*)
½ cup semolina (*sooji*)
1 tbsp oil
oil for frying

DAL PASTE
1½ cups *moong dhuli dal*
¾ cup *urad dhuli dal*
1½ tsp salt

FILLING
¼ cup cashewnuts - chopped
¼ cup *chironji*
¼ cup raisins (*kishmish*) - chopped
6-7 tbsp grated dry coconut (3" piece of coconut)

OTHER INGREDIENTS
500 gms curd
1 tbsp roasted cumin (*bhuna jeera*) powder
1 tsp red chili powder
1 tsp salt or to taste
1 cup sweet tamarind (*imli*) chutney
2 chopped green chilies
2 tbsp chopped fresh coriander
4 cups warm water with 1 tsp salt

1. Soak both the dals overnight.

2. Sift flour and semolina, add oil. Rub oil nicely into the flour with your hands to mix well.

3. Knead into stiff dough with warm water (1/3 cup approx.).

4. Roll out the dough into big round sized chapatti. Cut circles of 1½" from it. Roll out each circle to make it thinner and slightly bigger.

5. Heat oil in a *kadhai* and fry these small puris into golgappe. Put 5-6 pieces at a time and fry each batch for 2-3 mintures.

6. Grind the dal into a smooth paste in a mixer using about ¼ cup water. Add 1 tsp salt. Beat the mixture well for about 5-7 minutes with an electric hand mixer to get a soft paste.

7. Mix cashew, raisins, *chironji* and coconut together. Fill some of this filling into the golgappes by making small holes in it.

8. Heat oil in a *kadhai*. Dip golgappe into the dal batter and fry each batch for 4-5 minutes on low flame so that they get cooked properly. Fry all the golgappes.

9. Add salt in curd and mix well with a whisk. Before serving, put badas into the warm water squeeze with both hands. Arrange in a plate. Put curd, roasted cumin powder, red chilli powder and imli chutney over it.

10. Garnish with chopped green chilli and green coriander.

Veg Cutlet

Makes 9-10

1 cup boiled green peas
5 potatoes boiled, peeled and mashed (2½ cups)
6-7 (25 gms) French beans chopped finely
¾ cup finely chopped capsicum
1 cup finely chopped carrot
2 cups grated beetroot
2 green chillies - chopped
½ cup plain flour (*maida*)
4 tbsp cornflour
3 cups dry bread crumbs
1½ tsp salt or to taste
½ tsp red chilli powder
¼ tsp garam masala
½ tsp black pepper powder
¼ tsp soya sauce
oil for frying
1 tsp lemon juice
2 tsp butter

1. Boil water with ½ tsp salt. Add beans, capsicum and carrot, boil for 3-4 minutes. Take out from water. Put beetroot in the same water with ¼ tsp salt and boil for 3-4 minutes. Strain water.

2. Mix peas, potatoes, beans, capsicum, beetroot, green chilli, salt, red chilli powder, pepper powder, garam masala and soya sauce in a bowl. Mix nicely.

3. Heat 2 tsp butter in a non-stick pan. Add the mixture and sauté for 4-5 minutes on low flame. Let it dry, remove from heat and add cornflour.

4. Make a thin batter of ½-¾ cup water, flour, ½ tsp salt and ½ tsp red chili powder.

5. Make cutlets from the mixture. Dip in the batter and roll in bread crumbs.

6. Heat oil in a pan or *kadhai*. Fry cutlets till golden brown. Serve hot with tomato ketchup.

Noodle Rolls

Makes 14-15

100 gms noodles - boiled
3 tbsp grated cheddar cheese
1 green chilli - chopped finely, 2 tbsp chopped coriander
3 cups bread crumbs, ¼ tsp black pepper powder
¼ tsp red chilli powder, ¼ tsp garam masala
½ cup plain flour (*maida*), ½ cup water
¾ tsp salt or to taste
oil for frying

WHITE SAUCE
2 tbsp butter
2 tbsp plain flour (*maida*)
1 cup milk
¼ tsp salt
pinch of roughly ground black pepper

1. For white sauce, heat butter in a non stick pan. Add plain flour, saute for a minute. Remove from heat. Add milk, mix nicely so that no lumps form. Add salt, black pepper. Stir for 4-5 minutes on high flame. Let the sauce become thick stirring continuously. Remove from heat and let it cool.

2. Mix grated cheese, chopped green chilli, fresh coriander, bread crumbs, salt, garam masala, red chili powder and black pepper powder to white sauce. Add boiled noodles and mix carefully so that noodles do not break. Make rolls out of the mixture carefully. Make a thin batter of flour, water and salt.

3. Heat oil in a pan. Dip rolls in the batter and fry on low medium heat for 5 minutes or till golden brown. Serve hot.

Samosa

Makes 12

1 cup plain flour (*maida*)
3 tbsp oil
¼ tsp carom seeds (*ajwain*)
½ tsp salt
¼ cup water

FILLING
2 big potatoes - boiled and peeled
1½ tbsp oil
½ tsp cumin (*jeera*) - crushed, ½ tsp fennel seeds – crushe
½ tsp coriander seeds - crushed
1 tsp salt, ½ tsp dry mango powder (*amchoor*)
½ tsp red chilli powder
1 green chilli - chopped
1 tbsp chopped mint leaves, 1 tbsp chopped coriander
oil for frying

1. Sift flour in a parat. Add salt & oil & rub between the palms to mix well. Add 5-6 tbsp c water & make a stiff dough. Knead the dough with wet hands for 2-3 minutes. Keep asid

2. For the filling, mash potatoes coarsely.

3. Heat 1 tbsp of oil in a *kadhai*. Add crushed cumin, fennel seeds and coriander seeds, saut for 30 seconds. Add mashed potatoes, salt, red chilli powder, dry mango powder, gree chilli, coriander and mint. Mix well. Saute for 2 minutes and remove from heat.

4. Divide the dough into 6 balls. Roll each ball into 4"-5" diameter chapatti. Cut it int 2 equal halves. Put some water along the straight edge of the semi circle. Join and pres together to make a cone.

. Place 1½ tbsp filling in the cone and press to close the samosa. Make 12 samosas in the same manner.

. Heat oil in a *kadhai* and deep fry 6 pieces at a time on a low heat till golden, for about 6-8 minutes.

. Serve with mithi chutney.

Chilli Gobhi

Serves 2-3

00 gms cauliflower - cut into 3/4" florets
capsicum-chopped finely
1 cup cornflour
2 cup plain flour (maida)
pinch of baking soda (mitha soda)
-6 green chillies - chopped finely
2 tsp red chilli powder, salt to taste

½ tsp ajinomoto, optional
½ tsp coarsely grounded black pepper
½ cup tomato ketchup
2 tsp soya sauce, 2 tbsp chilli sauce
½ tsp sugar
4 tbsp butter
oil for frying

1. Make a thin batter of flour, cornflour, soda, red chilli powder, 1 tsp salt, ½ tsp tomato ketchup, ½ tsp chilli sauce, ½ tsp soya sauce with ¾ cup water.

2. Heat oil in a *kadhai*. Dip cauliflower in the batter and fry for 4-5 minutes till golden. Keep aside.

3. Heat butter in a pan. Add green chilli and saute for 1-2 minutes. Add capsicum, black pepper and ajinomoto and sauté for 2-3 minutes.

4. Add the remaining tomato ketchup, chilli sauce, soya sauce and sugar and sauté for 1-2 minutes.

5. At the time of serving add cauliflower and cook for 2-3 minutes. Serve hot.

Vegetables

Mughlai Dum Aloo

Serves 4-5

2 cups (250 gms) baby potatoes – boiled & peeled
2 big tomatoes - pureed
2 tbsp tomato puree (ready-made)
50 gms khoya – grated (1/3 cup)
½ tsp turmeric (*haldi*) powder
1½ tsp salt
2 tbsp cream
2 tbsp curd
1 tbsp lemon juice
1 tsp chaat masala

PASTE (GRIND TOGETHER)
2 tbsp coriander seeds (*sabut dhania*)
½" piece of ginger
1 green chilli
½ tsp cumin seeds (*jeera*)
7-8 cashewnuts
2-3 black pepper corns (*saboot kali mirch*)
2 green cardamom (*chhoti elaichi*)
1 black cardamom (*moti elaichi*)
2 cloves (*laung*)
1-2 cinnamon (*dalchini*)
1-2 mace blades (*javitri*)
2 dry red chillies

TEMPERING
4 tbsp ghee
1 tsp mustard seeds (*rai*)

1. Mix all the ingredients of the paste in a bowl, soak in ¼ cup water for ½ an hour. Grind a smooth paste. Add ¾ cup water to make it thin.

2. Heat ghee in a pan. Add mustard seeds, when it splutters add the masala paste. Sauté for 3-4 minutes.

3. Add grated khoya, saute for 1-2 minutes. Add pureed tomatoes and tomato puree, turmeric salt and chaat masala and mix well. Saute for 5-7 minutes. Keep stirring continuously till oil separates. Now remove from fire. Let it cool completely.

4. Add curd and cream and mix well. Again keep on low flame and cook for 1-2 minutes.

5. Add potatoes in the masala and cook for 1-2 minutes. Put 2 cups of water and lemon juice to get a thick gravy.

6. Give a boil and cook on low heat for 2-3 minutes. Garnish with coriander leaves.

Note: If you want you can fry the potatoes and add to the gravy.

Khoya Baby Corns

Serves 2-3

100 gms baby corns
50 gms khoya – grated (¼ cup)
2 tbsp coriander (*dhania*) powder
¼ cup tomato puree (ready-made)
2 tomatoes – grated
½ tsp salt or to taste
½ tsp red chili powder
¼ tsp garam masala
¼ tsp sabzi masala
½ tsp dry mango powder (*amchoor*)
½ tsp turmeric (*haldi*) powder
2 tbsp cream
1 tbsp chopped fresh coriander

POPPY SEEDS (KHUS KHUS) PASTE
1 tbsp khus khus
1 tbsp magaz

TEMPERING
3 tbsp ghee
1 tbsp finely chopped ginger
1 tbsp finely chopped green chilli
1 tsp cumin seeds (*jeera*)
1 bay leaf (*tej patta*)

1. Boil baby corns in salted water for 2-3 minutes. Remove from water and keep aside.
2. Soak khus khus and magaz in hot water for 15 minutes and grind to a fine paste.
3. Heat ghee in a pan. Add cumin seeds, bay leaf, ginger and green chilli. Sauté for 1-2 minutes.
4. Add khus khus paste, saute for 1-2 minutes. Add tomato purée, chopped tomato, coriander powder, salt, red chili powder, garam masala, sabzi masala, dry mango powder, turmeric and khoya. Sauté for 1-2 minutes.
5. Add cream and cook till masala leaves oil. Add baby corns and cook for 1-2 minutes.
6. Add 1 cup water and cook till the gravy is thick. Garnish with chopped coriander leaves.

Suman Special

Serves 3-4

6-7 big potatoes - boiled and chopped
2 big tomatoes - grated
4-5 ridge gourd (*tori*)
3 tbsp ghee, ½ tsp cumin seeds (*jeera*)
½ tsp red chilli powder, ½ tsp garam masala

½ tsp turmeric powder, ½ tsp dry mango powder
2 tbsp coriander powder
1 tbsp cream, 1 tbsp curd, 1 tsp salt or to taste

FOR POSTO PASTE (KHUSKHUS PASTE)
1 tbsp magaz, 1 tbsp poppy seeds (*khus khus*)
1 tbsp cashew nuts

1. Cut tori into big pieces. Boil in 2 cups of water for 7-8 minutes. Remove from water. Let cool and grind to a paste. Keep aside paste and water also.

2. Soak magaz, khus khus & cashew in hot water for 15 minutes & grind to a smooth paste.

3. Heat ghee in a pan. Add cumin. When it splutters add khus khus paste & saute 1-2 minutes.

4. Add tori paste and cook for 7-8 minutes on medium heat. Add tomatoes, salt, red chilli powder, garam masala, dry mango powder, turmeric, coriander powder, cream and curd. Mix well and cook for 8-10 minutes on medium heat till the gravy leaves oil.

5. Add boiled and chopped potatoes and cook for 1-2 minutes. Put some tori water to make thick gravy. Serve hot.

Note: After removing tori from boiled water, do not throw the water as you can use it to add in the gravy.

Jhatpat Paneer

Serves 2-3

100 gms paneer – cut into ¼" pieces
2 tomatoes – finely chopped
1 capsicum – cut into ¼" pieces
1 tbsp ghee
½ tsp cumin seeds (*jeera*)
½ tsp salt or to taste

½ tsp black pepper powder
1 tsp sugar
½ tsp garam masala
¼ tsp turmeric (*haldi*) powder
½ tsp dry mint (*poodina*) powder
¼ tsp green cardamom (*chhoti elaichi*) powder
2 tsp magaz (*melon seeds*) – roasted

1. Heat ghee in a pan. Add cumin and when it splutters add capsicum.

2. Add salt, pepper powder, sugar, garam masala, mint powder and turmeric and stir for 1-2 minutes.

3. Cover and cook for 5 minutes. Keep stirring in between. When capsicum is cooked, add tomatoes and paneer. Mix well and cook for 4-5 minutes on high flame. Keep stirring.

4. Remove from fire when the vegetable starts leaving oil. Garnish with roasted magaz and cardamom powder. Serve hot.

Veg Kofte

Serves 4

½ cup grated bottle gourd (*lauki*)
½ cup grated carrot
1 cup boiled and mashed potatoes
¼ tsp cumin (*jeera*) powder
1 green chilli – chopped finely
a pinch of baking powder
¼ tsp dry mango powder (*amchoor*)
¼ tsp garam masala
salt to taste
½ cup gram flour (*besan*)
2 tbsp butter
oil for frying

GRAVY

2 big tomatoes – chopped
2 tbsp tomato puree
¼ tsp turmeric (*haldi*) powder
½ tsp red chilli powder
½ tsp garam masala
1 tsp cumin seeds (*jeera*)
1 tbsp khus khus - soaked and ground to a paste
1 tbsp cream, 1 tsp curd
1 tsp coriander (*dhania*) powder
1 tsp salt or to taste
4 tbsp chopped fresh coriander
2 tbsp ghee

1. Mix *lauki*, carrot, potato, cumin powder, green chilli, baking powder, dry mango powder, garam masala and salt in a bowl.

2. Heat 2 tbsp butter in a pan. Add the above mixture and saute for 2-3 minutes. Remove from fire and cool.

3. In another bowl mix gram flour, ¼ tsp salt, ½ tsp red chili powder, and 1/3 cup water and make a thin batter.

4. Heat oil in a *kadhai*. Make walnut size balls from the mixture. Dip in the batter and fry for 3-4 minutes on medium heat till golden. Keep aside. (fry 5-6 kofta at a time)

5. Heat ghee in a pan, add cumin seeds. When it splutters add tomato puree, chopped tomatoes, salt, turmeric, red chilli powder, garam masala and coriander powder and saute for 5 minutes.

6. Add khus khus paste and sauté for 3-4 minutes. Add curd and cream and saute till it leaves oil.

7. Put ¾ cup of water to make a thick gravy so that it will coat the koftas. Give one boil.

8. To serve, cook gravy for 1-2 minutes and add koftas. Garnish with green coriander leaves and serve hot.

Goanese Aloo

Serves 3-4

5-6 big potatoes - boiled and chopped
2 cups tamarind pulp (soaks 2 walnut size tamarind balls in water and take out the pulp)
1 cup grated fresh coconut
a pinch of asafoetida (*hing*)
½ tsp mustard seeds (*rai*)
5-6 curry leaves
½ tsp fenugreek seeds (*methi dana*)
1 green chilli – chopped finely
1 tsp grated ginger
2 tbsp coriander chutney
1½ tsp salt
¼ tsp black salt
1 tsp jaljeera powder
1 tsp chaat masala
1 tsp chilli sauce
1 tbsp finely chopped fresh coriander
3 tbsp ghee

1. Soak boiled and chopped potatoes in tamarind pulp in a bowl for 2 hours.

2. Heat ghee in a pan. Add mustard seeds, curry leaves, fenugreek seeds, asafoetida, green chilli and ginger and saute for 1-2 minutes.

3. Take out potatoes from the tamarind pulp and add to the ghee. Add ½ cup of tamarind pulp also and sauté for 2-3 minutes.

4. Add salt, coriander chutney, chilli sauce, black salt, chaat masala, jaljeera and grated coconut. Saute for 7-8 minutes.

5. Add the remaining tamarind pulp. Cook for 5-7 minutes to get a thick gravy.

6. Garnish with chopped coriander leaves and serve.

Paneer Sinduri

Serves 4-5

200 gms paneer – cut into ¼" pieces
½ capsicum – cut into ¼" pieces
1 cup ready-made tomato puree
a small tomato – grated
3 tbsp butter
6-7 black pepper corns (*saboot kali mirch*)
¼ tsp carom seeds (*ajwain*)

1 tsp coriander (*dhania*) powder
½ tsp red chilli powder, ¼ tsp garam masala
½ tsp tomato ketchup
½ tsp paneer masala or tandoori masala
1½ tsp salt or to taste
1 tbsp chopped fresh coriander
1 tsp cream

1. Heat butter in a pan. Add carom seeds and saute for 1-2 minutes. Add grated tomato, tomato puree, salt and black pepper and sauté for 2-3 minutes.

2. Add capsicum, coriander powder, red chilli powder, garam masala, paneer masala, tomato ketchup and cream. Cook on low heat for 3-4 minutes or till the masala leaves oil.

3. Add paneer pieces and cook for 1-2 minutes.

4. Add little water to get a thick gravy. Give one boil and cook for 2-3 minutes on low flame. Garnish with green coriander and serve.

Navratan Korma

Serves 2-3

1 potato - boiled and cut into 12 pieces
1 carrot
1 capsicum
10-11 beans - cut into 2" pieces
1/3 cup peas - boiled
100 gms paneer - cut into small pieces
1-2 slices of tinned pineapple - cut into 1" pieces
2 big tomatoes - boil, peel and grind to a puree
½ tsp turmeric, ½ tsp red chili powder
½ tsp garam masala, 2 tsp coriander (*dhania*) powder
2 tbsp cream
5-7 cashewnuts - crushed, 7-8 raisins (*kishmish*)
4 tbsp oil/ghee
1½ tsp salt or to taste
2 tbsp coriander chutney (grind 4 tbsp coriander leaves with ¼ tomato)
1 tbsp finely chopped fresh coriander

FOR GINGER-GREEN CHILI PASTE (GRIND TOGETHER)
½" piece of ginger, 2 green chilies

1. Boil potatoes. Boil green peas.

2. Cut carrot and capsicum into 1" pieces. Boil carrot, capsicum and beans.

3. Heat oil in a pan. Add ginger-green chilli paste and saute for 1-2 minutes.

4. Add cashewnuts and sauté for 1-2 minutes. Add coriander chutney and saute fo 1-2 minutes.

5. Add freshly pureed tomatoes, cream, salt, red chilli powder, turmeric, garam masala and coriander powder. Sauté for 4-5 minutes on medium flame or till the masala leaves oil.

6. Now add all boiled vegetables, paneer, pineapple and raisins. Mix well. Add 1 cup o sufficient water to get a thick gravy.

7. Cook for 5-7 minutes. Garnish with coriander leaves.

Methi Malai Paneer

Serves 4

200 gms paneer - cut into 1½" long fingers
½ cup peas - boiled
1" cinnamon stick (*dalchini*)
3-4 cloves (*laung*)
2 black cardamom (*moti elaichi*)
1 tbsp cashewnuts - chopped
2 tomatoes - chopped finely
¼ tsp black pepper corns (*saboot kali mirch*)
¼ cup cream mixed with 3 tbsp cashewnut paste
3 tbsp dry fenugreek leaves (*kasuri methi*)
1 tsp salt
½ cup milk
a pinch of sugar
2 tbsp ghee
2 green chillies - chopped

FOR CASHEW NUT PASTE
Soak 4 tbsp cashewnuts in ¼ cup of water for
20 minutes, drain and grind to a fine paste

1. Crush together cinnamon, black cardamoms and cloves to a powder.

2. Heat ghee in a pan. Put the cinnamon mixture into it. Saute for 1-2 minutes.

3. Add crushed cashewnuts and sauté for 1-2 minutes. Add tomatoes, green chilli, black pepper and salt and sauté for 3-4 minutes.

4. Add ½ cup water, dry fenugreek leaves, sugar, cashew paste and milk. Cook for 5 minutes or till the masala leaves oil.

5. Now add paneer and peas and cook for 2-3 minutes. Serve hot.

Mirchon Ki Sabzi

Serves 4-5

9-10 thick green chilies (*achaari mirch*)
6 potatoes – boiled and mashed
1 tsp salt or to taste
1½ tsp chaat masala
½ tsp dry mango powder (*amchoor*)
½ red chilli powder
¼ tsp garam masala
2 tbsp curd
1 tsp lemon juice
a pinch of black salt (*kala namak*)
½ tsp butter

GRAVY

4 tomatoes – boil in water for 3-4 minutes, peel and grind to a fine paste
½ tsp salt or to taste
a pinch of dry mango powder (*amchoor*)
1 tbsp curd
2 tbsp cream
¼ tsp red chili powder
¼ tsp turmeric (*haldi*) powder
¼ tsp garam masala
½ tsp chaat masala
2 tbsp ghee
1 tsp cumin seeds (*jeera*)
1½ cups water

1. Slit and deseed green chillies. Boil water in a pan. Put green chillies in the boiling water an~ remove from fire. Take out green chillies from water after a minute.

2. In a pan heat butter. Add potatoes, salt, chaat masala, dry mango powder, red chili powde~ garam masala, curd, lemon juice and kala masala. Sauté on low heat for 5 minutes t~ prepare a nice masala. Remove from fire and cool.

3. Fill each green chilli with this masala nicely.

4. For gravy, heat ghee in a pan, add cumin seeds. When it splutters add pureed tomatoes, salt, dr~ mango powder, garam masala, chaat masala, turmeric powder and red chili powder. Saute fo~ 7-8 minutes.

5. Add curd and cream. Saute for 2-3 minutes. If there is any filling remaining, add filling ir~ the gravy masala and mix well.

6. Sauté masala till it leaves oil. Add the stuffed green chillies and put 1 cup water to get ɛ thick gravy. Cover and Cook on low heat.

7. When the green chilies are cooked remove from fire and garnish with coriander leaves.

aneer Butter Masala

erves 3-4

50 gms paneer - cut into triangles
bay leaf (*tej patta*)
tbsp cream, 1 tbsp curd, 1 cup milk

ASTE

-8 lotus seeds (*makhane*) - fry in 1 tsp butter and
tsp oil for 1-2 minutes
" piece ginger
½ tsp cumin seeds (*jeera*)
green chilli - chopped roughly
0-11 cashewnuts
" piece cinnamon (*dalchini*)
tbsp poppy seeds (*khus khus*)
tbsp coriander seeds (*saboot dhania*)
tsp turmeric (*haldi*) powder
4 tbsp water
tsp salt, or to taste
4 tbsp butter
2 big tomatoes - boil in 2 cups of water for
3-4 minutes, peel and grind to a paste

. Put the fried lotus seeds and all the other ingredients of the paste in a bowl. Soak in 1/3 cup of warm water for ½ an hour. Grind to a paste.

. Heat butter in a pan. Add bay leaf and saute for 1-2 minutes.

. Add the prepared paste and sauté for 4-5 minutes on medium heat. Add pureed tomatoes and cook for 10-12 minutes

4. Mix cream and curd in a bowl and add to the masala. Saute for 2-3 minutes on low flame. Add salt and ½ cup milk and cook till masala leaves oil. Add paneer. Cook for 1-2 minutes.

5. Add remaining milk to get a thick gravy. Garnish with grated paneer and serve.

Curd Kofte

Makes 20-22 Koftes

KOFTA

½ kg curd, 100 gms paneer (1 cup) - grated
2 tbsp flour (*maida*), ¼ tsp baking powder
1 tsp salt - to taste, ½ tsp red chilli powder
½ tsp garam masala
4-5 green chillies - chopped finely
1 tbsp chopped coriander
1 tbsp chopped cashewnuts

GRAVY

1 tsp cumin (*jeera*), 1 tsp mustard seeds (*rai*)
200 gms tomatoes – boil, peel & grind to a puree
½ tsp turmeric (*haldi*) powder
½ tsp chaat masala, ¼ tsp black salt
½ tsp sugar, ½ tsp dry mango powder (*amchoor*)
¼ tsp black pepper corns
2 tbsp ghee, 2 tbsp cream

1. Hang curd in muslin clothe for 3-4 hours to drain out water completely.

2. In a bowl mix hang curd, flour, paneer, baking powder, salt, red chili powder, garam masala, green chili, green coriander and cashewnuts. Mix well.

3. Make small balls from the mixture. Heat oil in pan, fry koftas one at a time till golden brown.

4. Heat ghee in a pan. Add cumin & mustard seeds, when they splutter, add pureed tomatoes, salt, sugar, dry mango powder, turmeric, chaat masala, black salt & black pepper corns. Saute for 2-3 minutes or till masala leaves oil. Add 1½ cups of water & cook for 3-4 minutes.

5. At serving time, boil gravy and add cream. Add kofte to the gravy. Serve.

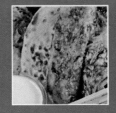

Parantha & Rice

Koki Parantha

Makes 4-5 paranthas

1 cup whole wheat flour (*atta*)
1 cup plain flour (*maida*)
2 tbsp finely chopped fresh coriander
2 green chillies - finely chopped
¾ cup finely chopped tomatoes
½ cup finely chopped cucumber
1 tsp cumin seeds (*jeera*)
1 tsp salt or to taste
2 tbsp melted ghee

1. Mix all the ingredient and add enough water to get a stiff dough. Knead well.

2. Cover with wet muslin cloth and keep aside for 10 minutes.

3. Make balls and roll out each ball lightly with a rolling pin (*belan*) into a parantha of about 5-6" diameter. Heat a griddle (*tawa*) on medium heat. Place the parantha. When the underside is cooked, turn to cook the other side. Smear some ghee or oil on the parantha and on the sides also. Turn and brown both sides. Similarly make other paranthas.

Coconut Rice

Serves 4-5

1 cup basmati rice - soaked in water for 15 minutes
1 cup grated fresh coconut
15-17 cashewnuts - chopped
¼ cup boiled *channa dal*
1½ tsp grated ginger
1 green chilli - chopped
2 tbsp oil
½ tsp red chili powder, ¼ tsp garam masala
1 tsp salt or to taste
½ tbsp lemon juice

1. Boil 4-5 cups water in a pan. Add 1 tbsp oil, soaked rice and ½ tbsp lemon juice. Cook till just done. Do not over boil. Remove from fire and strain the rice.

2. Spread rice in a big tray to cool completely.

3. Heat oil in a pan. Add ginger and green chilli. Sauté for 1-2 minutes. Add cashewnuts, grated fresh coconut, red chili powder, salt and boiled channa dal. Saute for 5-7 minutes.

4. Now add the rice and mix well carefully so that the grains do not break. Garnish with coriander and serve.

Fruit Rice

Serves 4-5

2 cups basmati rice – soaked for 15 minutes
2 cups or ½ tin mixed fruit cocktail – cut into small pieces
½ tsp red chilli powder
½ tsp black pepper powder
a pinch of garam masala
1 tsp salt or to taste
50 gms paneer – cut into small pieces

TEMPERING

2-3 cloves (*laung*)
1-2 green cardamom (*chhoti elaichi*)
1 bay leaf (*tej patta*)
1 tsp mustard seeds (*rai*)
3 tbsp oil

1. Boil 6-8 cups water in a pan and add ½ tbsp oil, add soaked rice and cook till the rice is just done.

2. When rice is cooked remove from fire and drain the excess water in a strainer. Spread rice on a tray and let it cool.

3. Heat oil in a pan, add mustard seeds, bay leaf, cloves and green cardamom. Sauté for 1-2 minutes.

4. Add chopped fruits, red chilli powder, black pepper powder, garam masala and salt. Saute for 3-4 minutes. Add cooked rice and mix well gently, without breaking the grains. Cook for 3-4 minutes.

5. Garnish with grated paneer and serve.

Baked Rice

Serves 5-6

2 cups basmati rice
1 capsicum – finely chopped
2 carrots – finely chopped
15-16 beans – finely chopped
1 tin (2 cups) baked beans
2 cheese cubes – grated and add 1 tsp oil, mix well.
1½ tsp salt or to taste
½ tsp black pepper powder
½ tsp garam masala
4 tbsp tomato ketchup
1 tsp chilli sauce
½ tsp soya sauce
¼ tsp black pepper powder to sprinkle on top

TEMPERING

5 tbsp oil
½ tsp mustard seeds (*rai*)
1 bay leaf (*tej patta*)

. Boil 6-8 cups water in a pan. Put beans and carrots in boiling water. Remove after 1 minute and keep aside. Add 1 tbsp oil to the boiling water. Add soaked rice and cook till just done. Do not over cook.

2. Strain the rice when cooked. Spread in a tray and let it cool.

3. Heat oil in a pan. Add mustard seeds and bay leaf. Sauté for 1-2 minutes.

4. Put capsicum, carrots, beans, salt, black pepper and garam masala. Saute for 3-4 minutes.

5. Add baked beans, tomato ketchup, chilli sauce and soya sauce, saute for 5-7 minutes. Remove from fire and keep aside.

6. Grease a baking dish. Put one layer of rice and one layer of the bean mixture. Again put one layer of rice and one layer of the bean mixture.

7. Spread grated cheese on it. Bake at 200°C for 7 minutes. Sprinkle black pepper powder on top and serve hot.

Mughlai Parantha

Makes 4

2 cups plain flour (*maida*)
1 tsp oil
1 tsp salt

POTATO FILLING

½ cup boiled and grated potatoes
½ tsp red chilli powder
1 tsp lemon juice
1 tsp chaat masala
½ tsp dry mango powder (*amchoor*)
½ salt or to taste

PANEER FILLING

½ cup grated paneer
1 tbsp finely chopped fresh coriander
a pinch of black pepper powder
¼ tsp garam masala
¼ tsp salt or to taste
¼ tsp red chilli powder
1 tsp finely chopped ginger
1 tsp finely chopped green chilli

OTHER INGREDIENTS

6 tbsp dhania chutney
6 tbsp tomato ketchup
4 tbsp red chili sauce

1. Sieve flour in a paraat. Add salt and oil, knead into soft dough by adding ½ cup of water. Keep aside for ½ an hour.

2. Make twelve balls of walnut size. Cover 8 balls and keep aside. Roll out 4 balls with a belan into thin chapattis. Cook each on a tawa from both the sides. Keep these 4 chapattis covered in a casserole.

3. Heat 1 tsp ghee in a pan add all the ingredients of potato filling and sauté for 4-5 minutes till it gets light brown in color. Keep aside and let it cool.

4. Heat another pan. Add all the ingredients of paneer filling sauté for 2-3 minutes.

5. Now roll out chapattis with remaining 8 balls. Don't cook these chapattis.

6. Take one uncooked chapatti, spread 1½-2 tbsp of potato filling.

7. Spread chilli and tomato sauce on one side of cooked chapatti. Put this side on the potato filling on the uncooked chapatti.

8. Spread dhania chutney on the other side of the cooked chapatti. Now spread 1½-2 tbsp of paneer filling on this side of chapatti. Spread little water on the edges of another uncooked chapatti, and put this chapatti on the paneer filling. Press it so that it will stick properly. Now you have one cooked chapatti covered on both sides with uncooked chapattis.

9. Cook this 3 layer parantha on a griddle from both the sides properly. Now make remaining paranthas and serve hot.

Methi Tamatar Pulao

Serves 3-4

2 cups basmati rice
3 tbsp dry fenugreek leaves (*kasoori methi*)
4 big tomatoes – finely chopped
½ capsicum – finely chopped
2 tsp salt or to taste
2 tbsp coriander (*dhania*) powder
½ tsp red chilli powder
¼ tsp garam masala
½ cup tomato ketchup
½ tsp chilii sauce

TEMPERING

5 tbsp oil
½ tsp mustard seeds (*rai*)
½ tsp cumin seeds (*jeera*)
1-2 dry red chillies

Boil 6-8 cups water in a pan with ½ tbsp oil. Add rice. Boil rice till done, but see that it does not get over cooked. Remove from fire.

Drain water from the rice. Leave in the strainer for 5 minutes. Spread in a tray and let it cool.

Heat oil in a pan. Add mustard seeds, cumin seeds and dry red chilli. Sauté for 1-2 minutes.

Add capsicum and dry fenugreek leaves, saute for 5-7 minutes. Add tomato, salt, red chilli powder, garam masala and coriander powder and cook till the masala leaves oil.

Add tomato ketchup and chilli sauce. Sauté for 2-3 minutes. Add cooked rice and mix well for 2-3 minutes. Serve hot.

Tiranga Parantha

Makes 4-5

3 cups whole wheat flour (*atta*)
3 tbsp oil
1 cup grated cauliflower (squeeze nicely)
½ cup finely chopped tomato
½ tsp cumin seeds (*jeera*)
salt to taste
a pinch of green food colour

1. Mix 1 cup flour, 1 tbsp oil, grated cauliflower, green food colour, ½ tsp salt. Add sufficier water and knead to a soft dough. Keep aside covered.

2. Mix 1 cup flour, 1 tbsp oil, 3 tbsp water, chopped tomatoes, ¾ tsp salt and knead to a so dough. Keep aside covered.

3. Mix 1 cup flour, 1 tbsp oil, 1/3 cup water, cumin seeds, ½ tsp salt & knead to soft dough.

4. Now make a rope from the three doughs and tie these into a plait (*choti*).

5. Make small balls from this plait and roll out each into a parantha. Heat a griddle and fr these paranthas from both the sides till golden. Serve hot.

Dhania Ke Paranthe

Makes 4-5

1 cup plain flour (*maida*), 1 cup whole wheat flour (*atta*)
4 tsp oil
1½ tsp salt or to taste
1 cup finely chopped fresh coriander
½ cup grated carrot, ½ cup grated paneer
1 tbsp gram flour (*besan*)
2 tsp cumin (*Jeera*) powder, ¼ tsp turmeric (*haldi*)
2 tsp finely chopped green chilli
¼ cup water

1. Sieve flour and wheat flour in a parat. Add all the other ingredients and sufficient water to knead into a soft dough.

2. Make walnut size balls and roll into thin paranthas.

3. Heat a griddle (*tawa*). Cook paranthas from both the sides, then fry by putting 1 tsp of oil on each side till golden. Serve hot.

Darbaari Cheese Pulao

Serves 6

2 cups basmati rice
½ tbsp ghee
1 cup finely chopped tomatoes
¼ cup cauliflower – cut into 1½" florets
¼ cup boiled peas
½ cup carrots – cut into 1½" pieces
½ cup lotus seeds (*makhane*) - fry or saute in oil
2 cheese cubes – grated

MASALA

½ tsp red chilli powder
½ tsp garam masala
½ tsp cumin (*jeera*) powder
½ tsp black pepper powder
1½ tsp salt or to taste
1 tsp biryaani masala

TEMPERING

5 tbsp oil
¾ tsp cumin seeds (*jeera*)
2 green chillies – chopped
1 bay leaf (*tej patta*)

. Boil 6-8 cups water in a pan with ½ tbsp ghee. Drain rice and add to boiling water. Cook till just done. Do not over boil.

. Drain water from the rice. Keep in the strainer for 5 minutes. Spread in a tray and let it cool.

. Heat oil in a pan. Add cumin seeds, green chilli and bay leaf. Saute for 1-2 minutes.

. Add cauliflower and carrot, saute for 2-3 minutes. Add add masalas - red chili powder, garam masala, cumin powder, black pepper powder, salt and biryaani masala. Mix well and cook for 5-7 minutes. Add tomatoes and sauté for 3-4 minutes.

5. Add peas and fried makhane, cook for 1-2 minutes. Add cooked rice and mix well.

5. Sprinkle grated cheese and mix lightly for 1-2 minutes. Serve hot.

Desserts

Fruit Salad

Serves 8

1 tin (800 gms) fruit cocktail
250 gms curd – hang in muslin cloth for ½ an hour
100 gms thick cream
1 cup powdered sugar

1. Beat sugar and cream in a bowl, till fluffy.
2. Beat curd separately. Now mix curd and cream and beat well again.
3. Chop fruits and keep in salad tray.
4. Spread the curd and cream mixture over it. Chill and serve.

Rasgulla Pudding

Serves 6

big rasgullas
¼ cup fresh pomegranate (*anar ke dane*)
100 gms kesar pista ice cream
tbsp finely chopped pistachio
tbsp finely chopped almonds
½ cup chilled milk
tbsp khus khus syrup/kesar syrup/rooh afza

1. Squeeze rasgulla well so that no syrup remains in it. Cut into halves and make a small hole in the centre by scooping a little.

2. Fill 7-8 pomegranate seeds in the hole and arrange in a flat serving dish.

3. Put ice cream, milk, kesar syrup and rasgulla pulp in a grinder and grind 3-4 times. Pour on the rasgullas in the serving dish.

4. Garnish with pistachio and almonds and chill in the fridge before serving.

Falooda

Enjoy this falooda as a drink or dessert.

Serves 6

1 small pack of ready-made falooda
4 cups milk, 2 tbsp sugar
½ cup rooh afza, 6 scoops of vanilla ice cream
2 tbsp subja seeds or tukmalanga or basil seeds (black seeds when soaked in water which become slipper
and transparent)

1. Soak subja seeds in 1 cup milk. Chill the seeds in milk for about 30 minutes or even more
   till they swell.

2. Boil the falooda in water for about 5 minutes until soft. Drain and refresh with cold water.
   Mix 2 tbsp rooh afza. Keep covered in the refrigerator till serving time.

3. Add 2 tbsp sugar to the remaining 3 cups milk. Keep in the fridge to chill.

4. To serve, add the subja seeds to the chilled 3 cups of milk. Mix well.

5. Divide this into 6 glasses. Add 1 tbsp falooda in all glasses. Then gently pour 2 tbsp
   rooh afza in each glass, which being heavier will settle to the bottom.

6. Float a scoop of ice cream on top of each glass. Stir once gently. Serve.

Biscuit Pudding

Serves 4

6 marie biscuits
Aluminum foil

MIXTURE
4 tbsp milk
1 tbsp powdered sugar
2 tbsp drinking chocolate powder
1 tbsp coffee powder, 1 tbsp cocoa powder

PASTE
2 tbsp plain flour (*maida*)
8 tbsp icing sugar
2 tbsp drinking chocolate powder
6 tbsp white butter – softened

FOR GARNISH
glace cherries
almonds flakes

1. Put all the ingredients of the mixture in a bowl and mix well to get a pouring consistency.
2. Put all the ingredients of the paste in a bowl, mix well to get a thick paste.
3. Dip marie biscuit in the mixture and overlap one by one, 8 biscuits like a sandwich.
4. Apply paste on all sides of the biscuit well with the help of spoon. Wrap in aluminum foil from all sides.
5. Use the remaining Marie biscuits in the same way.
6. Keep in the freezer for 3-4 hours. When the biscuits are frozen properly then remove from foil and cut into four to get triangular pieces. Decorate with glace cherries and almonds flakes. Serve.

Herbs & Spices

Asafoetida
(Hing)

Bay Leaves
(Tej Patta)

Cardamom
(Chhoti Elaichi)

Cardamom, Black
(Moti Elaichi)

Carom Seeds
(Ajwain)

Green Chillies
(Hari Mirch)

Dry Red Chilli
(Sukhi Saboot Lal Mirch)

Red Chilli Powder
(Lal Mirch Powder)

Cinnamon
(Dalchini)

Cloves
(Laung)

Coriander Seeds
(Saboot Dhania)

Coriander Seeds Ground
(Dhania Powder)

Coriander Leaves
(Hara Dhania)

Cumin Seeds
(Jeera)

Black Cumin Seeds
(Shah Jeera)

Curry Leaves
(Kari Patta)

Fennel Seeds
(Saunf)

Fenugreek Seeds
(Methi Dana)

nugreek Leaves, Dried
(Kasoori Methi)

Garam Masala Powder
(Garam Masala)

Garlic
(Lahsun)

Ginger
(Adrak)

Mace
(Javitri)

Mango Powder, Dried
(Amchoor)

Melon Seeds
(Magaz)

Mint Leaves
(Pudina)

Mustard Seed
(Sarson)

Nigella, Onion Seeds
(Kalaunji)

Nutmeg
(Jaiphal)

Peppercorns
(Sabut Kali Mirch)

megranate Seeds, Dried
(Anardana)

Sesame Seeds
(Til)

Saffron
(Kesar)

Turmeric Powder
(Haldi)

Brown Mustard Seed
(Rai)

Poppy Seeds
(Khus-Khus)

BEST SELLERS BY

Biryanis & Pulaos

Baking Recipes

All Time Snacks

Corn & Pasta - Vegetarian

Drinks & Indian Desserts

Tiffin Recipes for Children

New Chinese

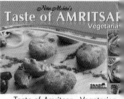
Taste of Amritsar - Vegetarian

Vegetarian Curries

Eggless Oven Recipes

Tikka Seekh & Kebab

Taste of Hyderabad - Vegetarian